D1424306

NF

Management Shapers is a comprehensive series covering all the crucial management skill areas. Each book includes the key issues, helpful starting points and practical advice in a concise and lively style. Together, they form an accessible library reflecting current best practice – ideal for study or quick reference.

The Chartered Institute of Personnel and Development is the leading publisher of books and reports for personnel and training professionals, students, and all those concerned with the effective management and development of people at work. For full details of all our titles, please contact the Publishing Department:
tel. 020-8263 3387
fax 020-8263 3850
e-mail publish@cipd.co.uk
The catalogue of all CIPD titles can be viewed on the CIPD website:
www.cipd.co.uk/publications

decision making and problem solving

and problem solving

JOHN ADAIR

Chartered Institute of Personnel and Development

© John Adair 1997

First published in the *Training Extras* series in 1997
First published in the *Management Shapers* series in 1999
Reprinted 2001

Design by Curve
Typesetting by Paperweight
Printed in Great Britain by
The Guernsey Press, Channel Islands

British Library Cataloguing in Publication Data
A catalogue record for this book is available from the
British Library

ISBN
0-85292-807-6

Chartered Institute of Personnel and Development, CIPD House,
Camp Road, London SW19 4UX
Tel.: 020 8971 9000   Fax: 020 8263 3333
E-mail: cipd@cipd.co.uk   Website: www.cipd.co.uk
Incorporated by Royal Charter. Registered charity no. 1079797

contents

Other titles in the series:

introduction

Not so very long ago, Hoover, the household appliance company, introduced a 'free flights' promotional scheme as an incentive for buying their products. It was a spectacularly bad decision. Some 200,000 people flew with the scheme, but it cost the company some £48 million. Some 127 people sought compensation in the courts, facing Hoover with a possible bill of millions of pounds if they succeeded. The president of Hoover Europe was dismissed from his £500,000-a-year post, and the American owners quickly sold the company for a knock-down price. You do not get decision-making more wrong than that.

Why did this fiasco happen? Because the Hoover managers concerned made a *false assumption*. They assumed that when most of the people who bought appliances saw the small print wrapped about the 'free flights' offer – the complex restrictions and qualifications they deliberately built in to deter applicants – these new customers would soon be daunted and lose interest in flying around the world. Not at all! Enough people pursued the incentive to bring the company to its knees.

This true story is a parable to remind us of the importance of decision-making and problem-solving in business leadership.

As Roy Thompson, one of the greatest businessmen of our time, once said, 'If I have any advice to pass on, as a successful man, it is this: if one wants to be successful, one must think; one must think until it hurts.' He added that, 'From my close observation, I can say that there are few people indeed who are prepared to perform this arduous and tiring work.' Are you one of them?

In the following pages we shall explore some practical ways in which you can improve your skills in this key area. By the time you have worked through the book you should:

- understand the way in which the mind works and the principles of effective thinking

- have a clear framework for decision-making

- be aware of the relation between decision-making and problem-solving

- be able to use a unified model for both making decisions and solving problems

- sharpen up your creative thinking skills

- be in a position to chart a way forwards for improving your thinking skills across the board.

1 your mind at work

Behind your practical, everyday thinking as a manager there lies the most complex thing in the known universe: the human brain. Nobody hires and pays you nowadays for your physical strength. You are employed because you have a brain – and can use it effectively.

There are two aspects to the brain: the information it can store in the memory, and what it can do. What we call technical or professional knowledge usually involves both. You not only need knowledge about a subject but you also need to be able to apply it in a variety of unforeseen situations.

Such applications of professional knowledge invariably involve decision-making and problem-solving actions. A doctor, for example, is problem-solving when he or she tries to diagnose the cause of your weak left leg. Indeed, decision-making and problem-solving are so bound up with particular kinds of information or knowledge – areas of professional competence – that we find it hard to think of them in the abstract.

Are there any generic or transferable skills in these areas? Yes, I believe there are. The characteristic function of the brain is to think. So let's leave on one side for a moment the memory or database function of the mind and concentrate on its primary role as a thinking tool. What is the nature of thinking? Are there any universal principles? If so, how can you use these principles to sharpen your skills as a practical thinker?

Is your brain working now?

Your brain has about 10,000 million cells in it. In fact it has more cells than there are people on the face of the earth! Each one can link up with approximately 10,000 of its neighbours, which gives you some 1 plus 800 noughts of possible combinations.

Our *potential* brain power is far greater than the actual power it achieves. No one has remotely approached the limits of it. One estimate suggests that we use no more than about 10 per cent of our brain power. So don't be worried by the fact that you are losing 400 brain cells every day – unless you do not exercise your mind much, in which case your brain will shrink at a faster rate. Use it or lose it!

There is a useful distinction between brain and mind. Take a computer as an analogy. Your brain is what you see if you open up the back of the computer – all those chips and circuits – whereas the mind is what appears dynamically on the screen. In this book we are focusing on the mind, for that is accessible to us without peering into the skull.

Before we go any further, I suggest we double-check that all your 10,000 million brain cells are warmed up and working properly by trying to solve some problems. Actually, the three problems below require only about 3,000 million brain cells, so they will not take long or cause us much delay!

Two other points before we begin. The three problems are not just brain-teasers: they illustrate principles about thinking. So I am not playing games with you. Secondly, I am not going to give you the answers in this chapter to the first two problems, though I shall do so later. This can be a bit frustrating. But I have a reason for leaving you in suspense. For reasons I shall explain later, I believe that the answers to both – assuming you cannot solve them immediately – may come to you later.

Problem 1   The nine dots
Take a piece of paper larger than this page and put on it a pattern of nine dots, like this:

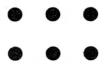

Now connect up the dots by four straight consecutive lines (that is, without taking your pen or pencil off the paper). You should be able to complete this task within three minutes.

Problem 2   The six matchsticks

Place six matchsticks – preferably of the wooden variety – on a flat surface. Now arrange the matchsticks in a pattern of four equilateral (ie equal-sided) triangles. You may not break the matchsticks – that is the only rule. Again, you should be able to do it within three minutes. There are at least two solutions, but I want the best one.

Problem 3   Who owns the zebra?

Having got the two easy ones safely behind you – well done if you have solved both those problems – we come now to something a little more demanding, so you must call up your reserve brain cells.

The world record for solving *both* parts of this problem is 10 minutes. So I will give you 30 minutes which, I am sure you will agree, is overgenerous of me!

1   There are five houses, each with a front door of a different colour, and inhabited by people of different nationalities, with different pets and drinks. Each person eats a different kind of food.

2   The Australian lives in the house with the red door.

3   The Italian owns the dog.

4   Coffee is drunk in the house with the green door.

5   The Ukrainian drinks tea.

6 The house with the green door is immediately to the right (your right) of the house with the ivory door.

7 The mushroom-eater owns snails.

8 Apples are eaten in the house with the yellow door.

9 Milk is drunk in the middle house.

10 The Norwegian lives in the first house on the left.

11 The person who eats onions lives in the house next to the person with the fox.

12 Apples are eaten in the house next to the house where the horse is kept.

13 The cake-eater drinks orange juice.

14 The Japanese eats bananas.

15 The Norwegian lives next to the house with the blue door.

Now, who drinks water and who owns the zebra?

The metafunctions of the mind

Let's now look at how the mind works. I suggest that there are three metafunctions: analysing, synthesising and imagining, and valuing. (That prefix 'meta' simply means more comprehensive, or transcending the lesser functions or skills of the mind.)

In the applied forms of effective thinking – decision-making, problem-solving, and creative or innovative thinking – all three of these metafunctions are at work. It is their underlying health that largely determines the quality of your thought. Few people have them in harmonious balance, as shown in the illustration below. Most of us are better at one rather than the other two. (There is some evidence that the modes are located in different sides of the brain, but that is beyond the scope of this book.)

The metafunctions of the mind

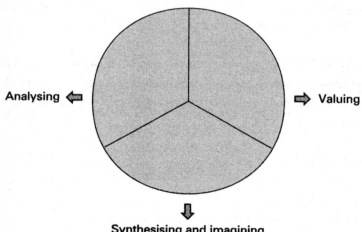

Analysing ⇦   ⇨ Valuing

⬇
Synthesising and imagining

Our differing mental strengths are a powerful reason why we need each other: effective thinking in all its forms is both a solitary and a social activity. You should always see yourself alternately as thinking alone (for yourself) and as thinking with others – either face to face or, as in this case, by reading or some other method of communication. Still, it is a good idea to seek to develop your skills in the weaker areas, like a person building up muscles in a limb through exercise: you will not always have the right people at hand to correct your bias towards a particular metafunction.

Analysing

The word 'analyse' comes from a Greek verb meaning 'to loosen', and it means separating a whole into its constituent parts. In tackling the *Who owns the zebra?* exercise you were using your analytical skills of dissection, trying to break down the task into its parts.

Analytical thinking is closely related to logical or step-by-step reasoning. You may have noticed that one of the skills you were using in tackling that particular problem was your power of deduction.

Logic has two main parts: deduction and induction. 'Deduction' means literally to subtract or take away. It is the process of deducing a conclusion from what is known or assumed. More specifically, it is a question of inferring from the general to the particular. 'All swans are birds. This is a swan. Therefore...' 'Induction' works the other way round. It is the process of inferring or verifying a general law or principle from the observation of particular instances – the core of the 'scientific method'.

Exercise 1
Spot the fallacy

Can you spot the logical fallacy in the following statement?

The chief executive of St Samaritan's Hospital Trust cleared his throat and began.

'Thank you all for coming to this meeting, which is, as you know, about how to improve the quality of our service in this hospital. To begin with I have decided to sack all the surgeons and physicians over the age of 55 years. Look at these letters! I have had five letters of complaint about the abruptness and lack of communication of doctors here, and two mentioned that the doctors are too old or have passed their "sell-by" date. The way to deal with this problem is to lower the average age of the staff, so I am going to ask everyone to take voluntary retirement at 55. Any questions before we move on to the next item on the agenda – litter in the corridors?'

For the main part, unlike the manager in the spot-the-fallacy exercise (see above), most of us are quite good at analysing problems or situations. This is not surprising, as much of our education is concerned with developing our deductive/inductive powers (mathematics, sciences, history, and literature) and sharpening our analytical skills.

You may now like to look at the solution to the *Who owns the zebra?* problem (see page 69). As you will see, it combines a test of your powers of reasoning or logical thinking with the important principle of trial and error. When you are faced with two alternatives – such as two roads at a junction without signposts that lead in the right general direction – there is no other way but to try each one in turn. In the case of this exercise, using a computer would save you time. But in real life you may, as they say, have to 'suck it and see'. Decision-making is not an exact science.

Synthesising and imagining

It is not easy to give a single label to the second metafunction. 'Synthesising' – another Greek word – is putting or placing things together to make a whole. It is the reverse process of analysing. You can synthesise things with your hands, which you do whenever you assemble or make anything. All products and services are the results of syntheses. But you can also do it mentally. When that happens, another faculty is called into play – imagination. Now, imagination works in pictures, and a picture is a whole that is more than the sum of its parts. If you shut your eyes for a moment and think of your house or your car, you see a picture. In fact, it is almost impossible not to see a picture. Your computer-like memory flashes it up on the inner screen of your mind very quickly. What you see is neither a pile of bricks, in the case of your house, nor a heap of car components, but in each case a whole.

If, so to speak, you turn up the volume knob of your imagination, you can see things that do not exist. Imagine, for example, a 56-metre-tall man... This road takes us into creative thinking, the subject to be explored more fully in Chapter 4.

The link between creativity and the synthesising process is clear when you contemplate how nature works. A baby arrives whole and it grows. Nature is *holistic*. A famous South African, Field Marshal Jan Smuts, who was also a keen agricultural scientist, coined this word to describe the process of creating wholes by ordering or grouping various units together. The essential realities in nature, Smuts argued, are these irreducible wholes. If analysed into parts, they lose their essential holistic quality. Your mind has a holistic dimension. It can think holistically – in terms of wholes – as well as analytically (taking wholes to bits).

Valuing

The third metafunction comes into play in such managerial activities as establishing success criteria, evaluating, appraising performance, and judging people – as in a selection interview. 'Criticism' (from the Greek word for a judge) is a form of valuing.

In all valuing there is an objective (outside yourself) element and a subjective one. We are all born with the capacity to value. What we *actually* value – our values – depends very largely upon our environment and its culture.

'Values' are rather like colours. What is the colour of grass? 'Easy,' you reply. 'It is green.' But scientists tell us that it has no intrinsic colour: it is merely reflecting light in the wave band that we call green. The structure of our eyes is also a factor. Our subjective contribution to the perception of colour is significant. Being colour-blind to certain shades of the red–green spectrum, I am personally very aware of that fact.

The word 'value' comes from a market metaphor: it is what you have to give in order to receive something across the counter. The invention of money revolutionised bartering. One merit of money is that it was a universal measuring-stick. But there are plenty of other values that enter into managerial decision-making these days. (See Exercise 2.)

Exercise 2
Values at work

Make a list of all the values – apart from financial value (profit) – which might influence any business decision over the coming 10 years.

Check to see whether the organisation you work for has issued a statement of its corporate values. If so, obtain a copy and underline what you judge to be the master-value in it.

How far do your organisation's values overlap with your own philosophy of life?

Whether or not values in the popular sense have a separate existence, and where they come from if not from ourselves, are philosophical questions that lie beyond the scope of this book. But in all thinking there is a strong case for acting *as if* truth – one member of the trinity of goodness, truth, and beauty – really does exist 'out there'. It would be impossible, for example, to explain the immense success story of modern science without the working belief of scientists such as Einstein that the truth is 'out there' waiting to be discovered.

The depth mind principle

As we all know, we have subconscious and unconscious minds. But we are not so aware of the vital part that these dimensions – I call them the depth mind – play in our thinking. You can actually analyse, synthesise, and value in your sleep or when you are consciously doing something quite different, like gardening or washing the dishes. Far from being chaotic, the depth mind plays a large part in scientific discovery and creative art. It is also the source of intuition – that all-important sixth sense.

Case-study

Conrad Hilton was trying to buy an old Chicago hotel. A few days before the deadline for sealed bids, Hilton submitted a bid for $165,000, a figure he had reached by some hasty calculations, as he was busy on other things at the time. He went to bed that night feeling vaguely disturbed and awoke the following morning with the feeling that his bid was not high enough. Another figure kept coming to him out of his depth mind – $180,000. 'It satisfied me. It seemed fair. It felt right. I changed my bid to the higher figure on that hunch. When the envelopes were opened the closest bid to mine was $179,000.'

Can you think of a similar decision or problem in your experience when your depth mind has played a similar role?

Check-list: Listening to your depth mind

	Yes	No
Do you have a friendly and positive attitude to your inner brain? Do you *expect* it to work for you?	❏	❏
Where possible, do you build into your plans time to 'sleep on it', so as to give your inner brain an opportunity to contribute?	❏	❏
Do you deliberately seek to employ your depth mind to help you to:		
◉ analyse a complex situation	❏	❏
▣ restructure a problem	❏	❏
△ reach value judgements?	❏	❏
Have you experienced waking up next morning to find that your unconscious mind has resolved some problem or made some decision for you?	❏	❏
Do you see your inner brain as being like a computer? Remember the computer proverb: 'Garbage in, garbage out.'	❏	❏
Do you keep a notebook or pocket tape-recorder at hand to capture fleeting or half-formed ideas?	❏	❏
Do you think you can benefit from understanding how the depth minds of other people work?	❏	❏

Roy Thompson, in his autobiography *After I Was Sixty* (1975), explains how it works. 'When a new problem arose, I would think it over and, if the answer was not immediately apparent, I would let it go for a while, and it was as if it went the rounds of the brain cells looking for guidance that could be retrieved, for by the next morning, when I examined the problem again, more often than not the solution came up right away. That judgement seems to have come to me almost unconsciously, and my conviction is that during the time I was not consciously considering the problem, my subconscious had been turning it over and relating it to my memory.'

2 the art of effective decision making

In decision-making there is a classic five-step approach which you should find extremely helpful. That does not mean you should follow it blindly in all situations. It is a fairly natural sequence of thought, however, and so even without the formal framework you would tend to follow this mental path. The advantage of making it conscious is that it is easier to be swiftly aware when a step is missing or – more probably – has been performed without understanding or intention.

It is useful to think of the five steps on page 18 as five notes of music. Logically they should be played in strict sequence. But the mind darts about. The notes can be combined in different sequences and mental chords. Thinking is not a tidy process, but it should be done with a sense of order.

Define the objective

Do you know what you are trying to achieve? You do need to be clear – or as clear as possible – about where you want to get to. Otherwise the whole process of decision-making is obscured in a cloud. As the proverb says, 'If you do not know what port you are heading for, any wind is the right wind.'

The classic approach to decision-making

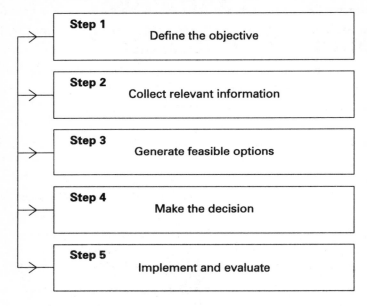

Step 1
Define the objective

Step 2
Collect relevant information

Step 3
Generate feasible options

Step 4
Make the decision

Step 5
Implement and evaluate

If you are in doubt about your aim, try writing it down. Leave it for a day or two, if time allows, and then look at it again. You may be able to see at once how it can be sharpened or focused.

Collect relevant information

The next skill is concerned with collecting and sifting relevant information. Some of it will be immediately apparent, but other data may be missing. It is a good principle not to make decisions in the absence of critically important information that is not immediately to hand, provided that a planned delay is acceptable.

Remember the distinction between *available* and *relevant* information. One classic mistake is to look at the broad decision and then turn to the information we have that will help us decide. Some managers do not, however, look at the information at their disposal and ask themselves 'Is this relevant?' Instead they wonder, 'How can I use it?' They are confusing two kinds of information – as is illustrated below.

Information categories

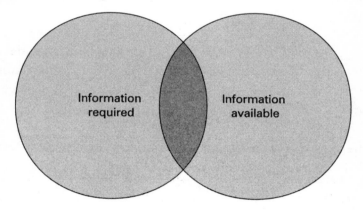

Life would be much simpler if you could just use the information at your disposal, rather than that which you really need to make the decision! So often quantities of data are advanced – information technology and the photocopier have a lot to answer for – that merely add bulk to a management report without giving its recommendations any additional (metaphorical) weight.

The rapid growth of methods of communication such as faxes, voice mail, electronic mail, junk mail and the Internet has now given us a new disease: Information Overload Syndrome. A recent international survey of 1,300 managers listed the new disease's symptoms, which included a feeling of inability to cope with the incoming data as it piles up, resulting sometimes in mental stress and even physical illness requiring time off work. The survey found that such overload is a growing problem among managers – almost all of whom expect it to become worse.

Executives and their juniors say they are caught in a dilemma: everyone tells them that they should have more information so they can make better decisions, but the proliferation of sources makes it impossible to keep abreast of the data.

The growth of information has been relentless. The *New York Times* contains as much distinct information every day as the average seventeenth-century person encountered in a lifetime. No wonder that half the managers surveyed complained of information overload, partly caused by 'enormous' amounts of unsolicited information. The same proportion also expected the Internet to become a prime cause of the problem over the following two years. To avoid succumbing to Information Overload Syndrome you need all the skills described in this book!

Suppose that the overlap between information *required* and information *available* is not sufficient: what do you do?

Obviously you set about obtaining more of the 'information required' category. But getting information or – to use a grander description – doing research incurs costs in time and money. Your organisation may not be in the business of making profits, but it certainly has to be businesslike when it comes to containing costs.

What the graph on page 22 suggests is that you usually acquire a great deal of relevant information in a relatively short time and, possibly, at a relatively low cost in money. But the line soon curves towards a plateau. You will find yourself spending more and more time to discover less and less relevant information. For example, if you and I sat next to each other at a dinner, I should learn all the really important things about you in the first half hour. The longer we talked, the smaller the increments of knowledge about you would become. After three hours I should be down to discussing relatively fine details.

Generate feasible options

Notice the word *options* rather than *alternatives*. An alternative is literally one of two courses open. Decision-makers who lack skill tend to jump far too quickly to the either–or alternatives. They do not give enough time and mental energy to generating at least three or four possibilities. As Bismarck used to say to his generals, 'You can be sure that if the enemy has only two courses of action open to him, he will choose the third.' Alfred Sloan, the renowned President of General Motors, was even known to adjourn meetings in which he was presented with two alternatives. 'Please go away and generate more options,' he would say.

The time/information curve

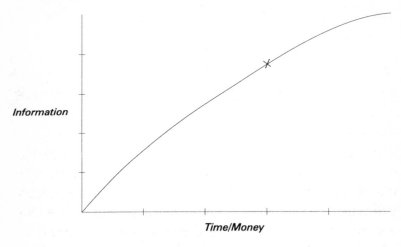

You need to open your mind into wide focus to consider all possibilities, and that is where creative thinking (see Chapter 4) comes in. But then your valuing faculty must come into play in order to identify the *feasible* options. 'Feasible' means capable of being done or carried out or realised. If it is feasible it has some real likelihood of being workable. It can attain the end you have in mind.

In moving along the Lobster Pot (see the illustration opposite) from the feasible options (no more than five or six, for the mind finds it difficult to handle more) to three options and then to two (the true alternatives), the principle to bear in mind is that *it is easier to falsify something than to verify it.*

The lobster pot model

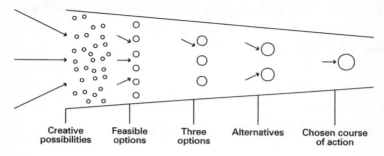

| Creative possibilities | Feasible options | Three options | Alternatives | Chosen course of action |

Suppose you are choosing between five medium-sized estate cars for your family. It is easy to eliminate the unsuitable ones. As you work on it, for example, you may discover that one of the cars is nine inches longer than the others, which will cause you a problem given the size of your garage. As for a second car, on studying the specifications you cannot see why it is £1,200 more expensive than the rest – apart from its prestigious name. So you drop that one too, leaving you now with three choices. You will notice another principle coming into play here, which (subject to the information/time curve) does take most of the pain out of decision-making. Let me continue with the car example.

Because your partner does not like the colours of the Toyota model and, being an artist by profession, feels strongly about it, you are able to eliminate that one. Your alternatives are now the Nissan and the Peugeot.

You have just read this book and so, being persuaded by its argument, you decide to trade some more time for some more information, and test-drive the alternative cars. Both feel great and perform really well. You know that either will serve your purpose. It is now a question of money and the availability of the colours your partner likes. One of the dealers offers you a much better price and can deliver the right model in the range. Why hesitate?

Make the decision

The critical preliminary activity here is to establish the selection criteria. It is worth dividing them into different levels of priority. (See the illustration below.)

Decision-making criteria

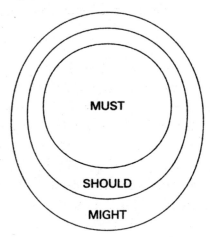

Unless an option meets the MUST requirements you should discard it. But after the essentials have been satisfied, the list of desirables – highly desirable SHOULDS or pleasant addition MIGHTS – comes into play.

Choosing a car is a relatively simple case, because there is a finite number of models to choose from and a relatively simple list of criteria. In order to help you choose in more complex cases, remember that you can make a decision by:

- listing the advantages and disadvantages

- examining the consequences of each course

- testing the proposed course against the yardstick of your aim or objective

- weighing the risks against the expected gains.

Assessing risk

What makes decisions really difficult is the factor of high risk. You may recall the conflicting advice of the two proverbs 'Look before you leap' and 'He who hesitates is lost.' There is an important skill in calculating risk. Calculation sounds mathematical, and there are plenty of management books with 'decision-making' in the title that offer various 'probability theories' and statistical methods to take the pain out of risk assessment. Sometimes it can help to assign numbers and calculate in that way, but the contribution of mathematics to this field is very limited. Experience plays a much larger part.

One helpful idea is to define the worst downside – what happens in the worst scenario? Can you accept that, or will it sink you? But in high-risk/high-reward situations, although you may know that you will be sunk if it does not all work out, you may still decide to take the high-risk course because the reward is just too important for you to forgo it.

You then have to address your mind to doing all you can to reduce the risk. It is here that experience, practice, consultation with specialists, reconnaissance, and mental rehearsals may all be relevant techniques. You are trying to turn the *possibility* of success into the *probability* of success, but you will not be able to eliminate risk altogether: in this situation there are too many contingencies.

Assessing consequences

Risk is one aspect of thinking through the consequences of the feasible courses of action.

Consequences come in two forms: *manifest* and *latent*. Manifest consequences are ones that, in principle, you can foresee when you make your decision. I say 'in principle' because that does not mean to say that you *did* foresee them. What I mean is that any reasonable person with the knowledge, experience, or skill expected of someone in your position would foresee those consequences. If you try to rob a bank, for example, the manifest consequences are obvious to any reasonable person:

- You might become amazingly rich.

- People, including you, might get hurt.

- You could be sent to prison.

Latent consequences are different in that they are not nearly so probable, or even possible, and a reasonable person might be forgiven for not seeing the knock-on effects that result from the complex chain of events triggered off by a decision. Admittedly, with the aid of computers it becomes a little easier in certain fields to identify latent consequences, but it is seldom possible to insulate yourself against pleasant or unpleasant surprises. We just cannot foresee the future in that way.

The emergence of latent consequences, of course, triggers off another round of decision-making and problem-solving activity. Yet solutions are the seeds of new problems. Introducing performance-related pay for individuals, for example, solves some motivational problems, but what other problems does it tend to create for teams and organisations, not to mention the individuals concerned?

Fill the quarters of the window in the illustration on page 28 with the consequences of a decision to make pay totally performance-related. Review the completed window – remember, you are looking for insights.

The outcomes window

	Positive	Negative
You		
Others		

I suppose that if we knew all the latent consequences of all our decisions at the time of making them, we should soon decide to stay in bed all day and never make another decision! But that decision in itself would have manifest and latent consequences... All that we can do, as humans and not angels or gods, is to make the best decisions we can, given the information and circumstances, and then make other decisions to deal with the manifest or latent consequences as they arise.

Implement and evaluate

Decision comes from a Latin verb meaning 'to cut'. It is related to such cutting words as 'scissors' and 'incision'.

The point of no return

Thinking   Action

Point of no return

What is 'cut off' in a decision is the process or activity of thinking. You now move into the action phase. Out with your cheque-book – start talking about delivery dates! Things begin to happen.

It is always worth identifying the Point of No Return (PNR), a term that comes from aviation. At the half-way point in crossing the Atlantic, it is easier for a pilot to continue to New York in the event of engine trouble than to turn back to London Heathrow. He has passed the PNR and he is committed.

In its wider sense the PNR is the point at which it costs you more in various coinages to turn back or change your mind than to continue with a decision that you now know to be an imperfect one. In most decisions you do have a little leeway before you are finally committed: you can still change your mind. Often, as in the case study of Conrad Hilton (see page 14), it is your depth mind that double-checks your decision and either whispers, 'Yes, I am satisfied' or begins an insistent campaign to make you at least review your decision, if not change your mind.

There is another reason for seeing implementation as part of the decision-making framework. Your valuing faculty is bound to come into play at some stage in order to evaluate the decision. Did you get it right? Could you have made the decision more quickly or more gracefully, perhaps at less cost to others? All this data goes into your memory bank and informs the depth mind, so that the next time you make a similar decision this information about your past may be available to you in the form of a more educated intuition.

Opening up the decision-making process to others

Remember that as a good manager – not a boss but a leader – you have to take your people with you. That means winning their commitment. That, in turn, means opening up those five boxes of decision-making (see the illustration on page 18) to your team: the more that people share in decisions which affect their working lives, the more motivated they are to carry them out.

Case-study

When Fort Dunlop was taken over by Sumitomo, the Japanese management asked for money-saving ideas from the workforce. A junior employee saved the company £100,000 a year in electricity payments by suggesting that every other fluorescent light in the huge factory did not need to be used – an idea that he had had for years!

The degree to which you as a leader can share decisions differs according to such factors as the situation – especially the time available – and the relative and relevant knowledge of the team members. Actually deciding where to decide on a continuum that has *control* at one end and *freedom* at the other is in itself an important decision when working with others. Here are some questions to ask yourself:

● Have you agreed the aims and objectives with the team?

■ Have you involved the team in the collecting and sifting of the relevant information?

▲ Has the team helped you to generate a number of possible courses of action?

● Have you used the synergy of the team members' minds to firm up the feasible options?

● Have you tested for consensus to see how far, in the circumstances, a course of action you favour is seen to be the optimum one?

- Have you secured everyone's commitment to make it work?

- Have you reviewed the decision with the team so that the lessons of success and failure are learnt for the future?

3 key problem solving strategies

Decision-making, problem-solving, and creative thinking have in common the fact that they are all forms of effective thinking. But there are some distinctions between them. You can, for example, think creatively, in the sense of having an original idea, without either making a decision or solving a problem. In this chapter the main focus is upon problem-solving.

How problems differ from decisions

What is a problem? A 'problem' is literally 'something thrown in front of you'. Another of those Greek words by origin, it is related to 'ballistics'. Originally what was thrown or put in front of one by the Greek teachers was the sort of puzzle or question that you encountered in the first chapter: the *Nine dots*, the *Six matchsticks* and *Who owns the zebra?* (Incidentally, has your depth mind come up with solutions – or extra solutions – to the first two yet?)

You will notice that in problems like these, all the elements of the solution are already there. All that you have to do is arrange or rearrange what has been given. In that sense, a problem is a solution in disguise.

As a result of solving such problems your life is not going to be different. By contrast, a decision usually *does* mean that life will be different. It opens the way to changes of some kind or other. Some of these changes are planned, wanted, expected or at least foreseen (the manifest consequences), whereas others are not. But solving or not solving a crossword puzzle is not going to change your life in any way.

In this respect such problems are similar to games – in fact, games are sets of problems. Why do we invent them? Because there is nothing that humans enjoy more than solving problems. The skills of a problem-solver in this limited sense, however, differ from those of a decision-maker. As a problem-solver you have to be clever, with analytical skills well honed on many other problems in that particular field. By contrast, a decision-maker needs a much wider range of skills and characteristics.

Moving away from puzzles and games, the problems we encounter in real life are mostly obstacles placed in front of us. If you decide to climb Mount Everest, for example, you may find that all goes well until – a day before your final ascent – a heavy storm suddenly develops on the South Col, the ridge leading to the summit. You have a problem! Notice that you would not have that particular problem – or any problems – on Everest unless you had made a decision to climb to the summit. It is not a problem for anyone else. And it would cease to be a problem for you if you changed your mind and decided to go off and climb some other mountain in the Himalayas.

Therefore problems as obstacles or difficulties in the path ahead of us are always secondary to the results of decision-making. Decisions create problems. One way of solving them – or rather the problem-state in your mind – is to alter your decision, or at least your plan. Did you have a contingency plan – a Plan B – for your route up the mountain if the weather deteriorated or avalanches (unexpected at this time of year) occurred?

If you stick with your decision, then, in consultation with your team, you have to find a way of overcoming the problem. Because the mental framework you must use is so similar to the decision-making process, a single model covering them both is possible.

A unified model for decision-making and problem-solving

If you are trying to cross a mountain stream you will jump from rock to rock, zig-zagging your way to the far bank. Like thinking inside your head, this is an untidy but purposeful activity. But when you have to get a team across a metaphorical river you need to be able to construct a simple bridge, so that everyone knows where they are in the decision-making/problem-solving discussion. (See the illustration on page 36.)

You can see that the skills required, as one phase merges into the next, change. A new metafunction with its family of more specific skills comes into play. The model is useful for your team as well as yourself. It can help everyone to keep in step.

The bridge model

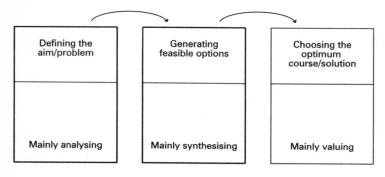

Asking the right questions

A key skill, both when you are thinking something through by yourself and when you are leading or participating in a team, is to *ask the right questions*. Questions are the spanners that unlock the mind. Here are the kind of questions you should ask yourself – and others.

Understanding the problem

● When did you first sense or become aware of the problem or the need for a decision?

■ Have you defined the problem or objective in your own words? (Remember that a problem properly defined is a problem half solved.)

▲ Are there any other possible definitions of the problem worth considering? What general solutions do they suggest?

● Are you clear about what you are trying to do? Where are you now and where do you want to get to?

● Have you identified the important factors and salient facts? Do you need to spend more time on obtaining more information? Do you know the relevant policies, rules, limitations, and procedures?

● Have you reduced the problem to its simplest terms without oversimplifying it?

Towards solving the problem

● Have you checked all your main assumptions?

▨ Out of all the possible courses or solutions, have you identified a short-list of the feasible ones?

▲ Can you eliminate some of these in order to shorten the list still further?

● If no solution or course of action seems right by itself, can you synthesise elements in two or more solutions to create an effective way of dealing with the problem?

● Have you clearly identified the criteria by which the feasible options must be judged?

● If you are still stuck, can you imagine yourself in the end-state where you want to be? If so, can you work backwards from there to where you are now?

■ Has anyone else faced this problem? How did they solve it?

Evaluating the decision and implementing it

● Have you used all the available information?

■ Have you checked your solution from all angles?

▲ Are you clear about the manifest consequences?

◉ Have you an implementation plan with dates or times for completion?

● Is the plan realistic?

● Do you have a contingency plan if things do not work out as expected?

■ When are you and your team planning to review the decision in the light of experience?

You may feel rather overwhelmed by this long list of questions. But you do not have to ask them all every time you are involved in making decisions or solving problems, for some of the questions will already have clear answers. What you should develop are three levels of competence:

● *awareness* of problems or the need for decisions – either actual or potential. Have your feelers out, so that you are not taken by surprise.

■ *understanding* of where you and the team are in relation to the problem or decision. In what phase of the bridge model (see page 36) are you? Does more work need to be done on analysing information and defining the problem or decision? Or are you in the business of generating feasible options?

▲ *skill* in asking the right questions of the right people at the right time, and being able to test the answers for their truth content. Action based on truth is much more likely to be effective than action based on a faulty perception of reality.

It may all sound like hard work. You recall Roy Thompson's words about 'thinking until it hurts' and 'this arduous and tiring work'. Yes, yes – but it is also great fun. It is what life is all about! I repeat: there is nothing more satisfying than being faced with a mental challenge and overcoming it. The harder the problem, the more elation you and your team will feel when you overcome it. So resolve to enjoy decision-making and problem-solving. The more you enjoy something the more of it you will want to do – and the better at it you will get.

How to approach systems problems

Obstacle-type problems account for 80 per cent of the problems that managers encounter, but you should also be aware of systems problems – the other 20 per cent.

A system is a whole made up of integrated parts. It can be organic (your body), mechanical (your car engine), or a process (your system for billing customers). A systems problem is essentially a deviation from the norm. We can represent it visually by two lines (see the illustration below). The greater the difference between the normal performance (how the system is supposed to work) and the active performance (what is actually happening), the bigger the problem.

Systems problems

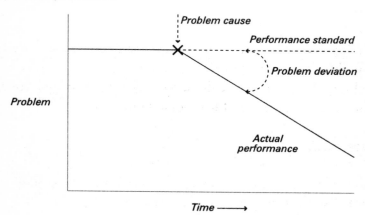

The main strategy in systems problems is to find the point of deviation and then establish what caused it. The first aim is to establish the exact time and place of that critical deviation. What happened? When? How much? Who was affected? Who saw it? And so on. Notice again that the key skill of asking the right questions is in play, focusing on the deviation point on the diagram.

Exercise 3
The W_5H Formula

Choose any systems problem facing you and practise your question skills – Who, What, Where, When, Why and How. See if you can pinpoint the deviation from the normal working of the system in question.

Once you have done that, list the possible causes. Now begin to eliminate the causes which can be proved innocent. You will be left with two or three suspects.

Having established when and where the deviation occurred, you then have to identify the cause or causes. Only by tackling these can you really solve a systems problem. Treat causes, not symptoms, if it is possible to do so.

Case-study

Plastec Ltd – a company making plastic containers – discovered that a rising percentage of its output was developing cracks. A project group studied the manufacturing process in detail and eventually defined the points of deviation: a change of supplier and a failure to clean out some storage vats. The new supplier inadvertently used these storage vats, and the plastic therefore became contaminated. Once the causes had been identified, the sytems were altered to prevent any repetition, and the problem did not recur.

Beware of the fallacy of the single cause. In relatively simple problems there is only one cause but, in more complex ones, two or three causes may be combining to produce the unwanted effect. In the case-study on Plastec Ltd you will have noticed that it was the combination of two changes from the norm – a new supplier and poor cleaning procedures – that produced the problem.

4 using creative thinking techniques

When you are stuck in problem-solving – that is, when the techniques you have applied successfully in the past are not working – try a more creative thinking approach. You may be trying to dig the same hole deeper, worrying at your problem like a terrier, when perhaps you should be digging your hole somewhere else.

Brainstorming

The best-known and most widely used creative thinking technique is brainstorming. It was introduced in the 1930s, so it has been around a long time – a sign of its usefulness. You can employ its principles when you are thinking alone, but they work better in a team setting.

When brainstorming, don't overlook the obvious! The obvious solution is sometimes the best. It may not, anyway, be obvious to everyone; and it may be possible to twist an obvious idea into something not so obvious. Don't fear repetition, either! Accusing someone of being repetitive is a form of adverse criticism and should be avoided. The same idea may trigger a different response at a different time in the brainstorming session.

Take the common paper-clip as an example. In five minutes one brainstormer came up with the following new uses:

Pipe-cleaner	Fuse wire
Nail-cleaner	Letter-opener
Tie-clip	Catapult missile
Ear de-waxer	Toothpick
Picture hook	Cufflink
Small-hole poker	Ornament
Screwdriver	Typewriter-cleaner
Fishing hook	Tension-reducer (like worry beads)
Broken bra-strap mender	Zip-fastener tag

I expect you can do even better than that! Are you ready to have a go? Look at the Guidelines opposite first.

Exercise 4
Brainstorming skills

Take a pair of scissors and list 50 new uses for them – apart from cutting things.

You have 10 minutes. Write your ideas down and – if stuck – go back and build on your first 10 ideas.

Guidelines for brainstorming

Suspend judgement	Give imagination the green light by withholding the critical evaluation of ideas until later. Accept ideas without judging them.
Welcome free-wheeling	Take off the brakes in your mind and go with the flow of your ideas. The more unusual the idea, the better – it is easier to tone down than think up.
Strive for quantity	The greater the number of oysters, the more likely you are to find some pearls in them.
Combine and improve	Listen to the ideas of others and see if you can build on them. Their way-out ideas may stimulate some buried memories or sleeping brain cells in your depth mind.
No editorialising	Ideas should not be elaborated or defended, just quickly stated and recorded.

One major reason why brainstorming is useful is that it helps to free us from 'functional fixedness'. We have a fixed idea, for example, that a thing has only one function and that is what it is there for. By banning the use of that familiar function (in the case of scissors, the function of cutting), the mind is released to consider other possibilities. With a little adaptation, scissors would make an interesting geometrical instrument... Take the modern British Army bayonet. Did you know that it is ingeniously designed to combine with its scabbard to form a pair of wire-cutters? Or that it has a third function (officially!) built into it – that of a bottle-opener?

Case-studies

Pilkington Brothers Limited in the UK had a technical problem... During the final inspection of sheet glass, small globules of water were identified by the inspection machine as flaws in the glass. A brainstorming session produced 29 ideas in less than five minutes. After research and development, three of these were used in the system, which solved the problem.

H J Heinz in the USA had a marketing problem... The company wanted to get sales promotional material to consumers more quickly. Brainstorming produced 195 ideas. After evaluation, eight were immediately used. A member of Heinz, when talking about another brainstorming session, said, 'Brainstorming generated more and better ideas than our special committee produced in 10 meetings.'

The essential principle behind brainstorming is simple. Please refer back to Chapter 1 and the three metafunctions of analysing, synthesising and imagining, and valuing. What brainstorming commands you to do is to make a temporary and conscious division between synthesising and imagining on the one hand, and valuing on the other – for much of our valuing is negative and premature, like unseasonable frost that kills off the buds of spring. As Jean-Paul Sartre once said, 'Criticism often takes from the tree caterpillars and blossoms together.' Brainstorming's suspension of judgement is an invitation to exercise some inner mental discipline. Analysing and valuing have their time and place, but your imagination has wings – let it fly free!

How to run a brainstorming session

No more than 10 people should be involved. Some may know about the field, others may not – a mixture of both is desirable. They should ideally have been trained in the brainstorming technique before the meeting.

- Define the problem (using your analytical and briefing skills).

- Help people to understand the problem by highlighting the background information and history.

- Clarify the aim in a succinct sentence: 'In how many ways can we...?'

● Have a brief warm-up session, using a common problem or object.

● Brainstorm 70 ideas in 20 minutes, or a similar target. One person should write up the ideas on a flip chart. Allow time for silent reflection. Check that no critical remarks are made. Encourage cross-fertilisation.

● Establish criteria for selecting the feasible ideas. Choose the best.

■ Reverse brainstorm: 'In how many ways can this idea fail?'

About 40 minutes is the optimum time for a brainstorming session. But you should ask the participants to go on considering the problem and let you have further suggestions. Remember that they have programmed their depth minds by the brainstorming session, and other ideas will come to them unexpectedly.

Case-study

A leading American firm of jigsaw-puzzle makers held a brainstorming session to think up ideas for new puzzles. It produced some worthy ideas but nothing brilliant. A month later, one of the participants went to see an exhibition of Tutankhamun's treasures in Washington DC. The gold mask of the pharaoh struck him as a great jigsaw-puzzle idea! He was right – it broke all records for jigsaw-puzzle sales in the USA.

Valuable though brainstorming is, not least as an introduction to one or two of the fundamental principles of creative thinking, it is not the whole story. To develop your skills as a creative problem-solver you need to adopt and practise the strategies set out below.

Towards a more creative approach

Brainstorming challenges one kind of unconscious assumption, namely that hammers are for knocking in nails or that scissors are for cutting. But there are other forms of unconscious assumption that may inhibit your thinking.

Take the *Nine dots* and *Six matchsticks* problems in Chapter 1. The reason why many people cannot do the first one is that they put an unconscious or invisible framework around the dots, and try to solve the problem within it. That is impossible. But if you break out of that self-imposed limitation, the solution to the problem is easily reached. (See the 'nine dots' solution on page 50.)

There is a similar assumption made in the second problem. People *assume* that they must arrange the six matches in a pattern of four equilateral triangles in only one plane. If they take one small step and give themselves permission to place the matches on top of one another, they can reach the first solution. But if they break out of the two-dimensional constraint into three dimensions, they achieve the most elegant solution.

The 'nine dots' solution

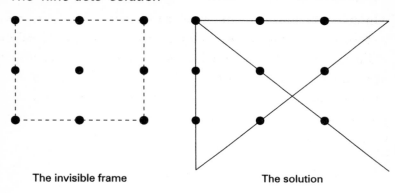

The invisible frame · The solution

The 'six matchsticks' solution

Star of David · Pyramid

Please don't mistake me: you cannot think without making assumptions. But they should be conscious ones from which you can retreat when they become indefensible. The assumptions that trip you up are the unconscious ones, the constraints or limitations that you are not aware of. That is one reason why effective thinking needs social interaction. We need our brothers and sisters to remove these filters from our eyes.

Look wider for solutions

In my early books on this subject I introduced the *nine dots* problem, and the phrase 'Think beyond the nine dots' or 'Think beyond the square' has now become a management proverb as a result. It ties in with 'lateral thinking', a phrase given wide currency by Edward de Bono. Lateral thinking means abandoning the step-by-step approach and thinking 'to one side'.

Vertical thinking	*Lateral thinking*
Chooses	Changes
Looks for what is right	Looks for what is different
One thing must follow directly from another	Makes deliberate jumps
Concentrates on relevance	Welcomes chance intrusions
Moves in the most likely directions	Explores the least likely directions

The sideways (or lateral) thinking involved often leads to reversing what appears to be the natural or logical way of doing things. For example, the earliest method of making cars involved teams of men moving from one car to another. Henry Ford turned it all upside down. He put the car frames on belts and moved them past the men – the birth of the assembly line.

It is important to think sideways because the seeds of a solution to a problem may lie outside the box you are working in. Really creative people have a wide span of relevance: they look far afield, even to remote places or times in history, for solutions to the problems they face. When the eighteenth-century agriculturalist Jethro Tull invented the seed drill he summoned up his previous experience as an organist: he was creatively transferring technology from one area to another. Most of us, however, tend to think in compartments, and the divisions in work that make specialisation possible encourage this blinkered thinking.

Case-study

Last year my 16-year-old son suddenly succumbed to GBS, a neurological disease that completely knocks out the peripheral nervous system, leaving the sufferer paralysed from head to foot. After seven weeks in an intensive care unit at a major London hospital, he was well enough to be transferred to a general ward. Here he was racked by chronic nausea. The specialists attributed it to the malfunction of the nervous system. As weeks went by, a second opinion was called for, which confirmed that diagnosis but said the boy's condition would get better, which, however, it did not. The stomach specialist did not seem to have any ideas – at least, none that worked. My son was now on a drip feed and various organs were beginning to suffer. Then a medical friend suggested I should contact a hospital specialising in spinal paralysis. The consultant there mentioned over the telephone two possible causes of nausea in paralysed people. One of them – decalcification of the bones – proved instantly to be the cause of my son's problem and was soon put right. The solution to the problem lay not in the *neurological* field or the *stomach* field, but in the *paralysis* area of competence. It was not to be found in the 'box' of one large hospital but in another, specialised, hospital 'box'. It required a degree of lateral thinking to find it.

How to be more creative

Creative thinking cannot be forced. If you are working on a problem and getting nowhere, it is often best to leave it for a while and let your subconscious – your depth mind – take over. Your mind does not work by the clock, although it likes deadlines. Sometimes the answer will come to you in the middle of the night.

Grasping the principle of the depth mind could open the way for you to a more creative approach to problem-solving. Many people are still not even aware that their depth minds can carry out important mental functions for them, such as synthesising parts into new wholes or establishing new connections while they are engaged in other activities.

Imagine your mind to be like a personal fax machine. It would be nice and tidy if you could sit down for an hour each morning before breakfast and receive inspired fax messages from your depth mind. But it is not like that. The fax machine might start whirring at any time of the day or night.

If you are thinking along a certain line and nothing happens, stop. Instead of investing more time – throwing good money after bad – analyse the problem again and see if you can come up with a new approach. Usually your frustration will be caused by one of the mental roadblocks described in the table on page 56.

The processes of analysing a problem or identifying an objective are themselves means of programming the mind. Possible solutions and courses of action almost instantly begin to occur to us. Where there is a time-delay this means that the deeper parts of the brain have been summoned into action and have made what contribution they can.

How important *preparation time* is for creative thinking! Careful and clear analysis, conscious imagining or synthesising (using such techniques as brainstorming either in groups or solo), and exercising the valuing function of thought in a positive rather than negative way – all these are vital to lay the foundations for thinking creatively. (See page 55.)

If you are planning to experiment and try a session before breakfast, it is useful always to have a preparation phase the night before. Imagine yourself as a house decorator, scraping down the woodwork and filling in holes and priming here and there, prior to painting a first coat the following day.

The creative thinking process

Preparation	The hard work. You have to collect and sort the relevant information, analyse the problem as thoroughly as you can, and explore possible solutions.
Incubation	This is the depth-mind phase. Mental work – analysing, synthesising and imagining, and valuing – continues on the problem in your subconscious mind. The parts of the problem separate and new combinations occur. These may involve other ingredients stored away in your memory.
Insight	The 'Eureka' moment. A new idea emerges into your conscious mind, either gradually or suddenly, like a fish flashing out of the water. These moments often occur when you are not thinking about the problem but are in a relaxed frame of mind.
Validation	This is where your valuing faculty comes into play. A new idea, insight, intuition, hunch, or solution needs to be thoroughly tested. This is especially so if it is to form the basis for action of any kind.

Mental roadblocks

Lack of facts	If you are not sure you have all the relevant facts, you naturally hesitate to commit yourself. Do some more research, and that may get you moving again.
Lack of conviction	Maybe you find it difficult because you lack conviction in the value of this exercise or the way in which you have been asked to do it. Re-establish a worthwhile objective.
Lack of a starting-point	Possibly the problem seems so large that you do not know where to start. If so, make a start anywhere. You can always change it later. Inspiration comes after you have started, not before.
Lack of perspective	Perhaps you are too close to the problem, especially if you have lived with it a long time or have been worrying about it incessantly. Try leaving it for a week. Consult others. Simply explaining it to them may help. They may see new angles.
Lack of motivation	Do you want it to happen enough? Creative thinking requires perseverance in the face of surmountable difficulty. If you are too easily put off, it may be a sign that, deep down, you lack the necessary motivation. Reinvigorate your sense of purpose.

The function of creative thinking in problem-solving is to come up with new ideas. But remember that at some stage your valuing skills have to be brought into play. Here are six questions to ask about any new idea, solution, or course of action:

- Is it really new?
- Is it both relevant and practical?
- Whom will it involve?
- How much will it cost?
- How much will it save?
- Will it require more formal evaluation?

In times of rapid change, like our own age, there is a premium on your skills as a creative thinker. If you can think productively and constructively, as well as analytically and logically, it will give you a third dimension in all your decision-making and problem-solving.

Exercise 5
Operation Brainpower

Two young managers come to you seeking advice on how they can develop their skills as decision-makers and problem-solvers. Having read this book, what programme would you suggest? How would you deepen their commitment?

Limit your programme to five action points. Be creative, for they are not interested in academic courses. See if you can invent an entirely new form of self-learning for them.

When you have worked out your programme, evaluate, using the six questions set out in the bullet list above.

Let me add the seventh big question: are you willing to try it on yourself? Please don't turn the page until you have completed this exercise.

Chartered Institute of Personnel and Development

Customer Satisfaction Survey

We would be grateful if you could spend a few minutes answering these questions and return the postcard to CIPD. <u>Please use a black pen to answer.</u> **If you would like to receive a free CIPD pen, please include your name and address.** IPD MEMBER Y/N

....

1. Title of book ....

2. Date of purchase: month ....   year ....

3. How did you acquire this book?
☐Bookshop   ☐Mail order   ☐Exhibition ☐Gift   ☐Bought from Author

4. If ordered by mail, how long did it take to arrive:
☐1 week   ☐2 weeks   ☐more than 2 weeks

5. Name of shop .... Town.. Country ....

6. Please grade the following according to their influence on your purchasing decision with 1 as least influential: (please tick)

	1	2	3	4	5
Title					
Publisher					
Author					
Price					
Subject					
Cover					

7. On a scale of 1 to 5 (with 1 as poor & 5 as excellent) please give your impressions of the book in terms of: (please tick)

	1	2	3	4	5
Cover design					
Paper/print quality					
Good value for money					
General level of service					

8. Did you find the book:
Covers the subject in sufficient depth   ☐Yes   ☐No
Useful for your work   ☐Yes   ☐No

9. Are you using this book to help:
☐In your work ☐Personal study   ☐Both   ☐Other (please state)

Please complete if you are using this as part of a course

10. Name of academic institution..

11. Name of course you are following? ....

12. Did you find this book relevant to the syllabus? ☐Yes ☐No ☐Don't know

Thank you!

To receive regular information about CIPD books and resources call 020 8263 3387.

1795/05/00

Publishing Department

Chartered Institute of Personnel and Development

CIPD House

Camp Road

Wimbledon

London

SW19 4BR

5 developing your thinking skills

Winston Churchill once said, 'I am always willing to learn, but I do not like being taught.' Actually, when you learn, you *are* being taught – by yourself. No doubt Socrates, if he was here, could teach you how to think, but he is not here. Nor is decision-making and creative problem-solving a school and university subject; there is no formal body of knowledge, supported by empirical research. And so, if you truly want to develop your thinking skills, your task is essentially one of self-development. In this chapter we shall look at some common-sense guidelines that you will need if you choose to go down that road.

What is an effective practical thinker?

Forming a clear picture of the kind of thinker you would like to be is the first step you need to take. A clear concept of what you might be one day can act as your magnet. Remember that point about formulating where you want to be and then working backwards?

You could do it in abstract terms, listing all the qualities, the knowledge, and the functions or skills you would like to acquire by such-and-such a date. I have to admit, though, that that does not work for me: it is a bit too academic. I suggest a more homely method, which any South Sea cannibal of olden times would have relished.

In Exercise 6 below I invite you to recall people whose thinking skills you have admired. They can be people you have known personally or have studied in some depth (by, say, reading more than one biography of them). In the right-hand column, write down as concisely and specifically as you can those thinking skills that impressed you and that you would like now to 'eat' by gobbling up and inwardly digesting, so that they become part of you. Write down, for instance, any key remarks or sayings by which the person concerned encapsulated his or her practical wisdom.

Exercise 6
Your personal thinking skill mentors

Name:	Thinking skill:

Take some time over this exercise, and try to get a good spread across the metafunctions (analysing, synthesising and imagining, and valuing) and the applied forms of effective thinking (decision-making, problem-solving and creative thinking). After all, you don't want to eat a meal composed of just one ingredient.

You will probably find it easy to come up with the names of two or three people – a parent, a friend, a life partner, or a boss you have worked for – who have exemplified a thinking skill that you covet. If it is not so easy, however, to complete the last boxes in Exercise 6, leave it for a week or two. Your depth mind will suggest other names and other lessons – influences that may have become more subconscious.

From your list of 'appetising' thinking skills you can begin to create a composite and imaginary picture of the perfect practical thinker. He or she would have A's analytical skills, B's rich and creative imagination, C's ability to be flexible and improvise, D's extraordinary judgement in situations of uncertainty and unpredictability, E's courage to take calculated risks, F's intuitive sense of what is really going on behind the scenes, G's lack of arrogance and openness to criticism, H's decisiveness when a decision is called for, and I's tolerance of ambiguity when the time is not ripe for a decision.

Now a perfect person with all these skills – a Mr or Mrs ABCDEFGHI – does not, and never will, exist. You may know the story of the young man who searched the world for the perfect wife. After some years he found her – but, alas, she was looking for the perfect husband! Perfection will always elude you – but excellence is a possibility.

What the exercise achieves, however, is to give you an ideal to aim for. Advanced thinkers in any field tend to be lopsided: like athletes, they develop one set of muscles rather than others. Did you know that sprinters are hopeless at long-distance running? I am not advocating that you should be a perfectly balanced thinker, a kind of intellectual 'man for all seasons'. Rather, I suggest you look carefully at your field and where you see yourself positioned in it in (a) five years' time and (b) ten years' time. The ideal that you formulate should be related to your field, although, of course, not all your personal thinking skill mentors will be from that field – at least I hope not, otherwise I should suggest that your 'span of relevance' needs widening.

Check that you are in the right field

Thinking skills are partly generic or transferable, and partly situational. Decision-making and problem-solving are not abstracts: they are earthed in a particular field, with its knowledge, traditions, legends, and values.

Dmitri Comino, the founder of Dexion plc, once discussed with me a book I was writing on motivation. 'In my experience,' he said, 'it is very difficult to motivate people. It is much better to select people who are motivated already.' The same principle holds good, I believe, for thinking skills. It is actually quite difficult to teach yourself skills that are not natural to you. So choose a field that suits your natural profile as a thinker. What is the right field of work for you? (See the table opposite.)

Key factors in choosing your field of work

What are your interests?	An interest is a state of feeling to which you wish to pay particular attention. Long-standing interests – those you naturally like – make it much easier to acquire knowledge and skills.
What are your aptitudes?	Aptitudes are your natural abilities, what you are fitted for by disposition. In particular, an aptitude is a capacity to learn or acquire a particular skill. Your aptitude may range from being a gift or talent to simply being above average.
What are the relevant factors in your temperament?	Temperament is an important factor. Some people, for example, are uncomfortable in decision-making situations of stress and danger, while others thrive on them. Some prefer to be problem-solvers rather than decision-makers.

It is usually easier to identify the fields that you are not suitable for, because you lack the necessary level of interests, mental aptitude, or temperamental characteristics to do really well in it.

Let me now make the assumption that you are in the right field. You have more or less the right profile of aptitudes.

You have been able, in other words, to acquire the knowledge and professional/technical skills needed and have enjoyed doing so. If the level you are now aiming for is a team leadership or management level, you have already laid the foundations of success. You will have credibility among your colleagues. Now what you have to do is focus upon the *process* skills – the more generic or transferable ones – in decision-making and problem-solving. How do you acquire them?

How to design your own learning strategy

Before planning your own self-learning programme it is useful to remind yourself of the core process of learning. (See the circle diagram below.)

How we learn

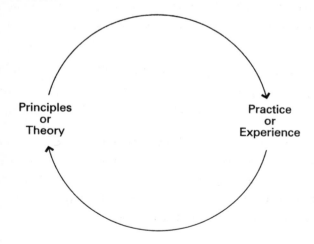

Principles
or
Theory

Practice
or
Experience

Recall what was said above about thinking skills being partly generic and partly situational. It is when sparks jump between these two poles that learning occurs. So you need both.

Because decision-making and problem-solving are such central activities in any person's life we have plenty of experience of them. And as you move into a professional field, and begin making decisions and tackling problems, you soon build up a repertoire of experience. You learn by mistakes. In the technical aspects of your work you do have a body of knowledge – principles or theory – to bring to bear on your practice. How can you apply the same learning method to thinking skills? Here are some practical suggestions:

- ● Read this book again and underline all the key principles. Put a star by the models or frameworks that you can use. Build up your own body of theory.

- ■ Make an inventory of your thinking skills in relation to your own field of work. What is the present profile of your strengths, and what are the areas for improvement?

- ▲ See if you can identify three outstanding decision-makers and problem-solvers in your field to whom you have access. Ask if you may interview them briefly to discover what principles – if any – have informed their own development as applied thinkers.

- Select one really bad decision made by your organisation during the last 18 months. Write it up as a case-study, limiting yourself to five key lessons to be learned about decision-making. If you want to develop your moral courage, send it to the chief executive!

- Now select any outstanding innovation in your field, inside your organisation or outside it. By an 'innovation' I mean a new idea which has been successfully 'brought to market' as a new (or renewed) product or service. Again, write it up as a case-study and highlight at the end the five or six key lessons for creative problem-solvers.

- Set yourself a book-reading programme. 'He would say that, wouldn't he!' But I do not have to persuade you to read books – you have just read this one. If you have enjoyed it, and found it worthwhile, try to read one general book each year on thinking (see *Further Reading* for some suggestions) and one biography of an outstanding person in your field. Again, underline the key principles in pencil. Surely you can budget time for one book in 52 weeks?

- Transfer your growing body of principles, examples, practical tips, sayings or quotations, and thumbnail case-studies to a stiff-covered notebook. As it fills up, take it on the occasional train journey or flight and read it reflectively, relating it to your current experience.

- ▲ Take any opportunities that come your way to attend courses or seminars which offer you know-how in the general area of effective thinking. You should, for example, become thoroughly versed in what information technology can do – and not do – at present in your field, and become skilled in the use of computers.

- Lastly, go out of your way to seek criticism of yourself as a decision-maker and problem-solver. However savage, however apparently negative the criticism, you still need it in order to learn. It is the toughest part of being a self-learner, but remember the sporting adage, 'No pain, no gain.' Your critics, whatever their motives or manners, are doing you the service of true friends. Sift through their comments for the gold-dust of truth.

In any self-learning programme, experience is going to play the major part. There is no getting away from that. But if you rely *just* on learning in what has been called 'the university of experience' you will be too old when you graduate to benefit much from the course! And the fees you will pay on the way will be extremely high. Short though it is, this book gives you those essential components – the key frameworks and principles – that you can use to cut down the time you take to learn by experience – experience and principles.

You will begin to develop both your knowledge of these process skills and your ability to apply that knowledge in all the challenging and potentially rewarding situations that lie ahead of you. Good luck!

appendix: solution to *who owns the zebra?*

This problem can be solved by analytical and logical thinking – deductive logic – and persistence! It is necessary to compile a matrix.

Roughly half-way through the problem-solving process there are two forks in the road, or mental leaps. The only way to find out which way to go is by trial and error. If you choose the wrong road, you have to retrace your steps. You can see now why the world record for finding the solution is 10 minutes!

This is one way of solving the problem:

Keep working through the facts from 1 to 15 in sequence.

Concentrate on clues for which there is only one answer. That is:

1   There are five houses, each with a front door of a different colour, and inhabited by people of different nationalities, with different pets and drinks. Each person eats a different kind of food.

9   Milk is drunk in the middle house.

10   The Norwegian lives in the first house on the left.

15 The Norwegian lives next to the house with the blue door.

Then look for information that has only two possible answers. This is the first mental leap. That is:

6 The house with the green door is immediately to the right (your right) of the house with the ivory door.

If you place the ivory door in the middle, with the green door on its right, the answer is wrong, but you can still progress to find out who drinks the water. However, you can go no further.

If you place the ivory door in the fourth house, with the green door on the far right, this answer is correct and you can progress logically, since you will find that other items of information now have only one answer. That is:

2 The Australian lives in the house with the red door.

4 Coffee is drunk in the house with the green door.

8 Apples are eaten in the house with the yellow door.

12 Apples are eaten in the house next to the house where the horse is kept.

Then look for information that has only two possible answers. This is the second mental leap. That is:

3 The Italian owns the dog.

If you place the Italian in the house with the green door you are wrong, but you can still find out who drinks the water.

If you place the Italian in the house with the ivory door you are correct and you can progress logically, since you find other items of information now have only one answer. That is:

5 The Ukrainian drinks tea.

13 The cake-eater drinks orange juice.

Therefore the Norwegian drinks water.

14 The Japanese eats bananas.

7 The mushroom-eater owns snails.

11 The person who eats onions lives in the house next to the person with the fox.

Therefore the Japanese owns the zebra.

Another way of solving this problem is to form a matrix using nationalities rather than house numbers:

Front doors	yellow	blue	red	ivory	green
Inhabitants	*Norwegian*	Ukrainian	Englishman	Italian	*Japanese*
Pets	fox	horse	snails	dog	*zebra*
Drinks	*water*	tea	milk	orange juice	coffee
Food	apples	onions	mushrooms	cake	bananas

further reading

ADAIR, J. *Effective Decision Making*. London, Pan, 1985.

ADAIR, J. *Effective Innovation*. London, Pan, 1996.

ADAIR, J. *Effective Leadership Masterclass*. London, Pan, 1997.

ALDER, H. *Think Like a Leader: 150 top business leaders show you how their minds work*. London, Piatkus, 1995.

DE BONO, E. *The Five Day Course in Thinking*. Maidenhead, McGraw-Hill, 1968.

DE BONO, E. *Lateral Thinking for Management*. Maidenhead, McGraw-Hill, 1971.

DE BONO, E. *Six Thinking Hats*. London, Penguin, 1985.

DE BONO, E. *The Use of Lateral Thinking*. London, Penguin, 1971.

BUZAN, T. *Use Your Head*. London, BBC Publications, 1974.

CULLIGAN, M. J., DEAKINS, C.S. *and* YOUNG, A.H. *Back to Basics Management*. New York, Facts on File, 1983.

DAWSON, R. *Make the Right Decision Every Time*. London, Nicholas Brealey, 1994.

DRUCKER, P. *The Effective Executive*. New York, Harper & Row, 1966.

DRUCKER, P. *The Practice of Management*. London, Heinemann, 1967.

KEPNER, C. H. *and* TREGOE, B. *The Rational Manager*. London, McGraw-Hill, 1965.

KOESTLER, A. *The Act of Creation*. London, Hutchinson, 1964.

RAWLINSON, J. G. *Creative Thinking and Brainstorming*. Aldershot, Gower, 1983.

With over 100,000 members, the **Chartered Institute of Personnel and Development** is the largest organisation in Europe dealing with the management and development of people. The CIPD operates its own publishing unit, producing books and research reports for human resource practitioners, students, and general managers charged with people-management responsibilities.

Currently there are some 150 titles covering the full range of personnel and development issues. The books have been commissioned from leading experts in the field and are packed with the latest information and guidance on best practice.

For free copies of the CIPD Books Catalogue, please contact the publishing department:

Tel.: 020-8263 3387
Fax: 020-8263 3850
E-mail: publish@cipd.co.uk
Web: www.cipd.co.uk/publications

Orders for books should be sent to:

Plymbridge Distributors
Estover
Plymouth
Devon
PL6 7PZ

(Credit card orders) Tel.: 01752 202 301
Fax: 01752 202 333

Other titles in the *Management Shapers* series

All titles are priced at £5.95 (£5.36 to CIPD members)

The Appraisal Discussion

Terry Gillen

Shows you how to make appraisal a productive and motivating experience for all levels of performer. It includes:

- assessing performance fairly and accurately

- using feedback to improve performance

- handling reluctant appraisees and avoiding bias

- agreeing future objectives

- identifying development needs.

1998 96 pages   ISBN 0 85292 751 7

Asking Questions

Ian MacKay

(Second Edition)

Will help you ask the 'right' questions, using the correct form to elicit a useful response. All managers need to hone their questioning skills, whether interviewing, appraising or simply exchanging ideas. This book offers guidance and helpful advice on:

- ● using various forms of open question – including probing, simple interrogative, opinion-seeking, hypothetical, extension and precision etc

- ■ encouraging and drawing out speakers through supportive statements and interjections

- ▲ establishing specific facts through closed or 'direct' approaches

- ● avoiding counter-productive questions

- ● using questions in a training context.

1998 96 pages   ISBN 0 85292 768 1

Assertiveness

Terry Gillen

Will help you feel naturally confident, enjoy the respect of others and easily establish productive working relationships, even with 'awkward' people. It covers:

- understanding why you behave as you do and, when that behaviour is counter-productive, knowing what to do about it

- understanding other people better

- keeping your emotions under control

- preventing others' bullying, flattering or manipulating you

- acquiring easy-to-learn techniques that you can use immediately

- developing your personal assertiveness strategy.

1998 96 pages   ISBN 0 85292 769 X

Constructive Feedback

Roland and Frances Bee

Practical advice on when to give feedback, how best to give it, and how to receive and use feedback yourself. It includes:

- using feedback in coaching, training, and team motivation
- distinguishing between criticism and feedback
- 10 tools for giving constructive feedback
- dealing with challenging situations and people.

1998 96 pages   ISBN 0 85292 752 5

The Disciplinary Interview

Alan Fowler

This book will ensure that you adopt the correct procedures, conduct productive interviews and manage the outcome with confidence. It includes:

- understanding the legal implications
- investigating the facts and presenting the management case
- probing the employee's case and defusing conflict
- distinguishing between conduct and competence
- weighing up the alternatives to dismissal.

1998 96 pages   ISBN 0 85292 753 3

Leadership Skills

John Adair

Will give you confidence and guide and inspire you on your journey from being an effective manager to becoming a leader of excellence. Acknowledged as a world authority on leadership, Adair offers stimulating insights into:

- recognising and developing your leadership qualities

- acquiring the personal authority to give positive direction and the flexibility to embrace change

- acting on the key interacting needs – to achieve your task, build your team, and develop its members

- transforming the core leadership functions such as planning, communicating and motivating into practical skills you can master.

1998 96 pages   ISBN 0 85292 764 9

Listening Skills

Ian MacKay
(Second Edition)

Improve your ability in this crucial management skill! Clear explanations will help you:

● recognise the inhibitors to listening

■ listen to what is really being said by analysing and evaluating the message

▲ interpret tone of voice and non-verbal signals.

1998 80 pages   ISBN 0 85292 754 1

Making Meetings Work

Patrick Forsyth

Will maximise your time (both before and during meetings), clarify your aims, improve your own and others' performance and make the whole process rewarding and productive. The book is full of practical tips and advice on:

- drawing up objectives and setting realistic agendas

- deciding the who, where, and when to meet

- chairing effectively – encouraging discussion, creativity and sound decision-making

- sharpening your skills of observation, listening and questioning to get your points across

- dealing with problem participants

- handling the follow-up – turning decisions into action.

1998 96 pages   ISBN 0 85292 765 7

Motivating People

Iain Maitland

Will help you maximise individual and team skills to achieve personal, departmental and, above all, organisational goals. It provides practical insights into:

- becoming a better leader and co-ordinating winning teams

- identifying, setting and communicating achievable targets

- empowering others through simple job improvement techniques

- encouraging self-development, defining training needs and providing helpful assessment

- ensuring that pay and workplace conditions make a positive contribution to satisfaction and commitment.

1998 96 pages   ISBN 0 85292 766 5

Negotiating, Persuading and Influencing

Alan Fowler

Develop the skills you need to manage your staff effectively, bargain successfully with colleagues or deal tactfully with superiors. Sound advice on:

- probing and questioning techniques
- timing your tactics and using adjournments
- conceding and compromising to find common ground
- resisting manipulative ploys
- securing and implementing agreement.

1998 96 pages   ISBN 0 85292 755 X

Working in Teams

Alison Hardingham

Looks at teamworking from the inside. It will give you valuable insights into how you can make a more positive and effective contribution – as team member or team leader – to ensure that your team works together and achieves together. Clear and practical guidelines are given on:

- understanding the nature and make-up of teams

- finding out if your team is on track

- overcoming the most common teamworking problems

- recognising your own strengths and weaknesses as a team member

- giving teams the tools, techniques and organisational support they need.

1998 96 pages   ISBN 0 85292 767 3